Frogs
For Kids

Amazing Animal Books
for Young Readers

by John Davidson
Mendon Cottage Books

JD-Biz Publishing

Read More Amazing Animal Books

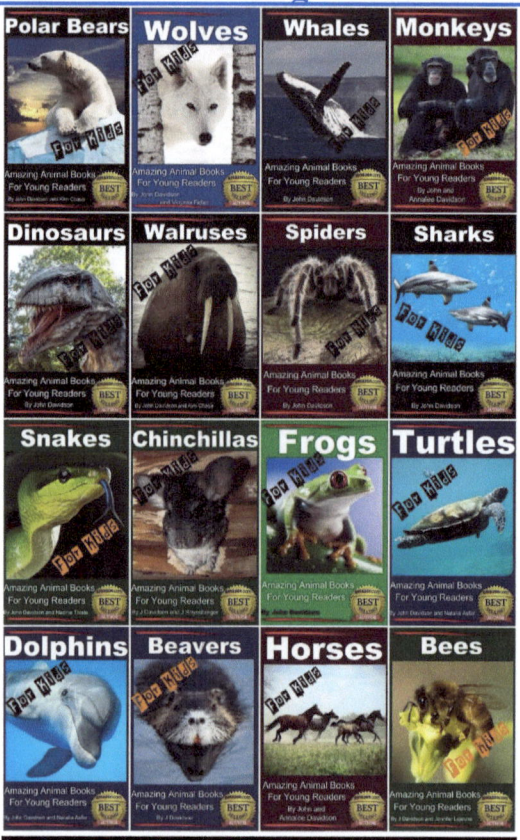

Purchase at Amazon.com

Download Free Books!
http://MendonCottageBooks.com

Table of Contents

1. Frogs: Fascinating Facts

Wherever you are, wherever you live…you will find frogs! These fascinating creatures live all over the world, except in the most frigid part of Antarctica. There are endless variations of size and color and they make the widest range of sounds. They even live in our most imaginative fairy-tale world and in ancient myths.

Frogs often turn into handsome men and beautiful princesses in fairy tales. Chinese mythology associates frogs with magicians and escape artists. In Scotland, you give images of them as gifts to new neighbors, to bring luck to their homes, and the ancient Egyptians claimed that frogs meant fertility and would bring a couple many children.

Generally speaking, frogs will gather around a water source in the early evening, especially when there is rain in the air and they will start to call; for a soul mate, their friends or just for the joy of hearing their own voices.

So, this evening, as the sun goes down, wrap up warmly, take a flashlight and go out of doors to your nearest pond, river or a grassy, damp place in your garden and listen…

<u>Fascinating Facts</u>. You will find more about all these facts as you read this book.

1. Frogs belong to the zoological class called **Amphibians** and are cold-blooded **vertebrates.**

2. There are about 3,900 different **species** of frogs, including toads. They are all born with tails but loose them, as they grow.

3. Common species of frogs include the Goliath frog; Darwin's frog; the Northern Leopard frog; the Poison Dart Frog; the Ornate Horned Frog; the Tree frog and the Wood frog.

4. Toads are basically the same as frogs, but they belong to a class called **Bufonidae.**

5. All frogs have flat heads, bulging eyes and strong hind legs, which are long and adapted for swimming and leaping. In general, frogs prefer a moist environment.

6. Some toads prefer a drier climate. Their legs are usually shorter and are adapted for walking more than leaping. Toads usually have warty, quite rough skins and are often poisonous.

Azure dart frog / Dendrobates azureus

7. Frogs do not need to drink water as they can readily absorb it through their skins.

8. The nose and the eyes of a frog are positioned on the head in such a way that allows it to breathe and see while the rest of its body is submerged under water.

9. There are some frogs which can jump further than **20 times** their body length, in one leap.

10. Frogs swallow their food whole. Mostly they eat the meat of bugs and worms. They help humans by getting rid of some pesky disease carriers.

11. The Goliath is the world's biggest frog. It lives in West Africa in Cameroon. It has a body that can measure more than one foot.

12. The smallest frog on earth used to be the Brazilian Gold frog. (Less than 1cm long). Last year, in 1912, an even smaller, (7mm) perfect frog was found in Papua New Guinea. It has a BIG name: ***Paedophryne amauensis.***

13. In Africa, Darwin's frog is adapted for carrying its tadpoles in its mouth until they turn into froglets…it is the male frog that performs this task!

Green Pond Frog © *photoncatcher36 - Fotolia.com*

14. **Herpetologists** are people who study frogs. **Herpetology** is the science of studying reptiles and amphibians. A frog hibernates each year, during which it forms a new ring in its bones. These rings, developed each year, are useful in determining the age of a frog.

15. Frogs like coming out during the rainy season.

16. There is a desert frog that can hibernate for up to 7 years. During this period, it encloses itself in a semi-transparent bag. It wakes up when the first rains come and eats the bag as its first food. Froggie fast food!

17. Frogs do not see colors; they only see black and white. Their pupils can take different shapes, such as heart-shaped or even square.

18. The Golden dart frog is the most poisonous frog on earth. A single Golden dart skin can kill over 1,000 people.

19. Scientists have discovered a painkiller that comes from the skin of a frog, that is 200 times more powerful than morphine.

20. Frogs only live in fresh water.

21. Most poisonous frogs in the tropics have bright colors to ward off potential predators.

22. Frogs breathe through their skin, lungs, and mouth.

23. Frogs do not have external ears. They have round, drum-like discs, called **tympanum,** flat on either side of their heads, just behind their eyes.

24. Only male frogs croak.

2. The Frog's Life Cycle.

Frogs reproduce just like human beings. They go through several stages of development in order to grow fully. Let's take a look at what happens throughout the life cycle of a frog.

Mating

When two frogs fall in love they mate. The male frog will embrace the female in a hug. He sits on top of her and holds her around the waist while she lays her eggs. This is called **amplexus** and can last anywhere from one day to seven days. This usually happens in water but it can also take place on land or even in a tree. The male frog is fertilizing the eggs that the female lays in this stage. Frogs lay thousands of single eggs in large bundles. This is called egg spawn and looks like a slippery, jelly-like mass. Frogs lay so many eggs to ensure that at least a few will survive. Many other creatures that live in the water, and even birds, like to eat frog eggs, so there is a real danger that they might all get gobbled up.

Toads mating close up © *egonzitter - Fotolia.com*

Eggs

Each egg will divide into two, four, and then six and so on.

The female will lay about 3 000 eggs and can you believe;

only 3-5 of those will survive? The eggs are usually laid in a calm stretch of water and they will bond together and create a layer of foam. This foam protects the eggs from drying out in the sun. Eggs hatch around 7 to 21 days after they have been fertilized and produce tadpoles.

Tadpoles

The tadpole lives off the yolk of the egg that is still attached to it's stomach. The tadpole only has a mouth, a tail, underdeveloped gills and is very fragile. At this point it is safer for them to attach themselves to weeds or other plants in the water for around a week. Once the week passes, they can safely swim around freely and eat algae in the water. It takes the tadpole 4 weeks to develop better gills that are covered by a thin skin. They will also develop small, ridge-like teeth to help them eat, and a better tummy system so that they can digest food easily. They are very sociable creatures and stick together in schools.

Common Frog, Rana temporaria tadpole with internal gills

© Eric Isselée - Fotolia.com

Tadpoles grow their limbs

After 6 to 9 weeks, the tadpole will get a more distinct head, grow long legs, and have a longer body. They can now eat plants and even small insects. The arms will be bulging at the sides and their elbows are the first to pop out. At this time, they look a lot like full-grown frogs, but with long tails.

Froglets

A young frog looks a lot like an adult but they still have a small, stubby tail behind them. It takes the froglets 12 weeks to get to this point and soon they will start to leave the water for adventures on land.

Frogs

By the time it is between 12 to 16 weeks, the frog is fully developed. It no longer has a tail and it will have strong and long back legs and shorter arms. It will also have developed a fine voice and will start calling for a mate, in order to start the process all over again.

Life span.

How long does a frog live? Are you surprised to know that this is a question we actually can't answer? It is very difficult to track a wild frog and nobody has ever done it, yet. So we have to go on the records of frogs in captivity. This seems to be anything between 3 – 17 years; with the longest record being a whopping 40 years.

3. Where Do Frogs Live?

When we talk about where frogs live, it is called their **habitat.**

Frogs are amphibians. That means they live can live on land and in the water. Frogs are usually born in the water and as tadpoles, they mostly feed on algae. As adults, they don't have to be in the water but they spend a lot of time there. They do not actually have to drink the water either, because they absorb it through their skin! Adult frogs live on plants and bugs and are just as at home on land.

Frogs are the most familiar group of amphibians. They live all over the world except in the very coldest regions of the artic and the very hottest and driest deserts. Something that helps them survive the extremes of climate is the fact that they are cold blooded. This means they will adapt to a very cold place by dropping their body temperature and, in a very hot land, the body temperature will be much higher.

Frogs a supremely adaptable and there are over 3,900 species. Some species who live in drier places, can store water in their bodies. They survive by living in underground burrows or buried in the mud of a pool that has dried out. Once kind of Australian frog has been known to survive 7 years without water!

Normally, frogs are happiest in wet places and this is where you will always find them. You will often hear them croaking, individually and in loud choruses, especially at night. This chorus is usually made up of mating calls, but frogs are able to sense the coming of rain and will sing out this message as well. In Asian countries, like India, their singing will cause great excitement among human beings as it heralds the coming of the life giving summer rains, called **the monsoon**.

Wet places often also get very cold and frogs have clever ways of surviving in colder climates In cold areas frogs use glucose or sugar in their bodies to increase tolerance to the cold to keep them from freezing.

One kind of frog that lives in North America stays frozen solid all winter and comes back to life when it thaws out! They can also hibernate in extreme conditions and we will talk about that in the next section.

Frog © *Gudellaphoto - Fotolia.com*

Frogs can make great pets! If you want to have a pet frog, you need to make sure you have the right habitat for your frog to live in. You will need to get a suitable **terrarium**. This is a glass container for keeping small animals. Check with the pet store or your vet, to make sure you know what size terrarium to get, what types of plants to put in it, and what types of bugs to feed your frog. You should have your parents' permission when getting a pet frog and they can help you make the right decisions in caring for it. Some frogs get really big and even eat mice! Your parents might not want you to have this kind of frog so, make sure about the kind of frog you get!

4. Hibernation

Frogs are cold blooded and this means that its body temperature will adapt to its habitat. This also means that it has a special trick for surviving the extreme cold of some of the places that it lives: hibernation.

toad © *Keith Paquette - Fotolia.com*

What is hibernation?

Hibernation is a specific period in an animal's life cycle when is sleeps through cold weather. This type of sleep is a bit different to the type of sleep experienced by humans. When a human sleeps, they can be awakened by loud noises and if someone shakes them. Animals in hibernation do not wake up even when moved around or touched. They will appear dead and may take a couple of months to wake up and start moving. Most hibernating animals will typically wake up when the weather starts warming up, particularly during spring, when there is plenty of food.

Do frogs eat during hibernation?

During the hibernation period most frog species that we know about do not eat. They depend on their stored up energy. All the bodily functions in the frog that require large amounts of energy slow down and sometimes, shut down altogether. During hibernation, their **metabolism** slows down to almost nothing. Metabolism is the work the cells in your body need to do, to make enough energy to keep you just alive. If humans tried to hibernate, they wouldn't last a week without food and water.

Frogs that live in water.

These are called **aquatic** frogs and they will typically hibernate under water. Unlike aquatic turtles, which burrow underneath the bottom of a pond or stream, aquatic frogs will only bury themselves partially or even lie on the bottom, sometimes even moving around very slowly, from time to time. This is because they still need to draw oxygen from the water to survive.

Frogs that live on land.

These are called **terrestrial** frogs and they burrow deep into the earth, to just below the frost line, where it is a bit warmer. Frogs who are not well adapted for digging, like tree frogs, prefer hibernating in deep crevices and cracks in logs and rocks. Some of these frogs even opt to hide deep in leaf litter where they are protected from cold temperatures. Some wood frogs are so well adapted for cold weather that they will actually allow 67% of their entire body to freeze. In the frozen state their metabolism is extremely low, they stop breathing, their heart stops pumping and brain activity comes to a standstill. The frog can remain this way for 2 or even 3 months. Amazingly, it will only take these tree frogs one to two hours to regain their normal state during springtime when it gets warmer.

Hibernation of frogs in captivity

For those who keep frogs as pets, it is important to help them maintain their natural characteristics and rhythms. Frogs will not hibernate if kept in normal house temperatures; they will only hibernate when introduced to the cold temperatures outside. As soon as autumn starts turning to winter, you should create a small terrarium outside for your frog. Ask your vet to advise you on what kind of environment you should build for it to have a happy hibernation period.

5. Are Frogs and Toads the Same?

Many kids have now gone for frogs as well as toads as their pets. They however keep on wondering how the two differ, because their appearance is much the same. This is because they are both amphibians. They are also both vertebrates and cold-blooded.

The development process for the frogs and toads is similar as they are born from eggs, live under water as tadpoles and then develop into adults. They both have vocal cords and an enormous variety of calls. They both have similar feeding habits and can survive on the same diet. In fact, they are pretty much one and the same thing, except for a few distinct differences.

The first thing that is very different is the skin. Frogs have moist, velvety skins and prefer to live very close to water and in a moist habitat. In general, their body shape is sleeker than that of a toad and the webbed feet are well developed for swimming. The toad tends to enjoy a drier habitat and its skin is drier, warty, and much harder to the touch. The toad is also a lot squatter and has a rounder body to look at, as its back legs are very well developed. This is because it loves to hop off on adventures overland.

African sand frog (Tomopterna cryptotis) on white © *EcoView - Fotolia.com*

Another difference comes out during the laying of eggs. Toads lay their eggs in a long chain in inhabited water or stagnant pools. They have an extremely nasty taste, and this protects them from being eaten by fish and other predators. Frogspawn on the other hand is produced in quieter water and in huge numbers. They are all stuck together in a jelly-like substance that looks almost like a patch of foam on the surface.

It is always best to be careful when choosing to have toads as pets. This is because some toads have a poisonous skin and we are advised against touching it. The frogs however are very safe and can be good playing partners. Having a frog or a toad can be a great idea and it requires you to build a suitable habitat where it can be happy. You can invite your friends to come and see them as they are awesome to look at it is fantastic listening to their croaking sounds.

6. What Do Frogs Eat?

Frogs are very interesting creatures who don't vaguely look like frogs at the start of their lives. Life for a frog begins when eggs are laid in a pond. The little eggs hatch into tadpoles that are herbivores, meaning they only eats plants, mostly the **algae** found all around them. Algae are tiny plant-like organisms that live in water. They do not have roots and leaves like ordinary land plants. The tadpoles start a change which is called a **metamorphosis,** by first growing long, hind legs and shorter front legs. As their gills disappear and their lungs develop, their digestive system also matures, allowing them to become **carnivorous**. Now they are able to eat small worms and insects as well. In the final stage of growth, the tail is absorbed into the rest of the body.

What do most adult frogs eat?

Well most frogs are carnivorous; this means that they eat other small animals. A good number of small frogs eat insects such as moths, dragonflies, mosquitoes, crickets and flies. Adult frogs will eat larger insects like grasshoppers, praying mantis, worms and snails. There are different species of frogs and some are larger than others. The larger species such as the bullfrog are capable of eating small reptiles and animals. Since these frogs are a bit bigger in size, they can eat lizards, mice, bats and smaller frogs as well.

Frog eating fish in a lake

It is easy for frogs to catch insects as their tongues are attached to the front of their mouths. They are long, sticky, and extremely mobile and lightning fast. The frog spots a delicious snack, rolls out its sticky tongue, wraps the tip around the prey, and then rolls the caught insect back into its throat. Zap, zap, just like that.

Frogs have no teeth so they have to swallow their prey whole. An interesting fact about frogs is that while swallowing, their large eyes sink into the openings of the skull, helping to force the food down the throat.

Frog catching fly with tongue © *Cathy Keifer - Fotolia.com*

There are also frogs who do not have tongues and they actually use the four fingers on each hand to catch the food and put it into their mouths.

Do other animals eat frogs?

Sadly, yes. Other larger animals eat Frogs. Snakes, dogs, foxes, rats, fish, bats, hawks, fish, turtles and seagulls are some of the many animals that consider frogs prey. In some countries, humans also eat frogs. Because frogs have many predators, certain species of frogs are good at **camouflaging** themselves to blend into their environment. This species of frogs can change the color of their skin depending on the surroundings to escape being noticed by predators. Unfortunately, their greatest enemies are humans. This is not because some people eat them as delicacies, but because we are slowly but surely destroying their habitat.

Frogs for pets

Frogs do make very good pets but they require a lot of care. They have to be fed regularly so that they can continue to grow. When you have a frog for a pet, you need to buy him insects to feed on from the pet store or worms from the fishing shop. You will also have to catch him a mouse occasionally as a special treat. They much prefer live food. It is quite difficult to train them to eat dead prey.

Please be careful if you catch food for him yourself. Be sure the bugs, insects etc, are not covered in pesticides, which might harm your pet.

Snake eating a frog

7. Types of Frogs

Colors.

There are many kinds of frog in every part of the world. They can be distinguished from each other broadly in several ways. The first, biggest difference is the color. Most frogs are green but this does not mean that all frogs are green. Some frogs are yellow, brown, black, orange or red in color and some frogs can even change color. Color also helps frogs to stay out of trouble, especially to avoid being seen by enemies who might want to eat them. Can you remember from the previous section how many bigger animals eat frogs? This is why frogs are experts at **camouflage** – just like our soldiers, and adventurers, who work in the wild, will wear clothes that blend into the natural colors of the area they are working in, so will some frogs assume colors indistinguishable from their background. These frogs are usually multi-colored. Some frogs can even change their shape to blend into the background even more cleverly.

Tomato frog / Dyscophus quineti

Calls.

Frogs can also be recognized by the kind of calls that they make. Certain frogs bark like a dog, while others seem to almost chirp and there is a whole range of different calls in between. Every different kind of frog has a unique call. There is an amazing variety of calls and it is easy to tell them apart. If you would really like to have some fun, then go to your local library or onto the Internet, and search for sound recordings of frog calls, especially listen to the sound of a bullfrog! Most frogs are calling for mates, or warning off predators or even calling for help from others of their kind. You can be sure that there will be a reason behind every call.

Special adaptations.

Certain frog types have very special body structures, like sticky pads that help them stick on the grass. This types of frog lives in grass and trees and are well camouflaged in those areas. In South America, there are frogs with small horns on their heads and large mouths. They are very aggressive and will hop towards you if you frighten them and they may even bite you. There is a species of frog named after the great explorer Charles Darwin, which has a very special adaptation. The male frog will collect the strongest tadpoles of his mate in a large pouch in his throat. He will protect them there until they grow into tiny froglets and then release them into a stream. There are tree frogs with extra large, red eyes that spend most of the time curled up, hiding their bright eyes. Once a predator approaches them, the frogs open their red eyes wide and stare at the predator, scaring it away.

Red-Eyed Tree Frog / Boophis luteus

Waxy monkey frogs are another type of tree frog. They climb trees and gasp the branches using their hands. They are called waxy, because they produce a waxy substance which they spread all over their body. This wax helps them to keep their skins moist, as they love to lie in the sun on the branches of the trees.

Another group of frogs is poisonous and we will tell you about them in the next chapter.

8. Poisonous Frogs as Pets

Pets make good company. However, you should always be cautious about the types of pets you keep at home. Some frogs are very poisonous and can harm you. One of the most popular poisonous pet frogs is the blue poison dart frog, which was discovered in Southern Surinam and Northern Brazil. This frog is extremely poisonous in the wild, however, it loses this venom once put into captivity. Its local Indian name is Okopipi and the hunters regularly use its virulent venom to poison the tips of their spears.

This dart frog is medium size and lives for about 6 years in the wild. Its brilliant blue color serves as a warning to predators and the alkaloid poison glands are located in its skin. The frogs can easily be identified by the unique pattern of the individual's black spots. Each foot contains four toes like most frogs, but the blue dart frog also has a suction pad on each toe, which helps it grip. Another characteristic is that it has a hunch-backed posture.

blue poison arrow frog - blue poison dart frog - d
© *Darren Green - Fotolia.com*

The major sources of food for this poisonous frog are termites, ants, caterpillars and beetles. The females are larger than the males and they actually do the fighting to win the males' attention. They will then settle as a couple, near some quiet water, where she will lay her eggs. The males will then fertilize the eggs externally and usually, the male takes care of the eggs, by defending his territory. The female will often feed the new tadpoles on unfertilized eggs.

This species is very hardy and make good pets. They are both territorial and aggressive and it is best to keep them in pairs. They are very active and need a large terrarium with land, trees and water. The atmosphere must be kept suitably humid and moist for them to be happy.

You will find more information on keeping frogs as pets in the section on Tree Frogs.

9. Poison Dart Frogs

Have you ever seen a poison dart frog? Have you ever wondered about them?

Poison dart frog

The scientific genus is **Phyllobates.** They are usually very small animals, but their poison is some of the most powerful in the animal kingdom. They are always brightly colored and have bold and striking patterns in blue, black, red and yellow. Their bright colors protect them by telling other animals that it would be dangerous to eat them. Dart frogs live in the Rainforest in Central and South America and they thrive in temperatures of 80 to 90 degrees.

This habitat is important to the frogs. They are provided with shade from direct sunlight which is not good for them. The poison dart frog hunts bugs during the day which they can do, because their brightly colored skin warns predators to avoid them. These animals eat small insects, especially ants and mites and it is the neurotoxic venom of their food source that makes them poisonous. The poison enters their bodies as part of the food chain and is then usually excreted through their smooth skins. When in captivity, they are usually deprived of their natural diet and most species will steadily become less and less poisonous to humans.

Most poisonous frogs are commonly called dart frogs because their venom is used to poison arrows used for hunting. People who live in villages near the habitats of the poison dart frog use their poison on the tips of darts and arrows. When the dart hits the animal that is being hunted, the venom causes it to loose consciousness and the villagers can then easily capture it.

Scientists have discovered that the toxin, or poison, found on the frog can have medical purposes. It can be used as a sedative and a painkiller. In some cases, it is many times more powerful than morphine. It would seem from on-going research that it also has less harmful side effects that many pain killers in use today. The very latest research suggests that it could also form part of a curative drug for serious diseases.

Dart frog / Ranitomeya benedicta

One of the problems for the dart frog is that its habitat, the Rainforest, is disappearing due to humans cutting down the trees for farms and lumber. Because the frogs are not well suited to living in other places, they have become endangered. This means that there is a chance that they could disappear from the animal kingdom. There are hundreds of types of these frogs, but only a few offers a serious threat to humans. One of these is the golden poison arrow frog, suitably named Phyllobates terribilis!

10. Tree Frogs

These are medium sized frogs with white stripes running down its sides. The female green tree frogs are 5-7 inches long and the males are 4-6 inches. They are native to the southeast parts of the USA. They are commonly found in the states of Florida, South Georgia, South Carolina etc. The green tree frogs are easy to keep and care for. They make a good pet. The following are some care and maintenance tips for Green tree frogs.

Green Tree Frog

Housing

Green tree frogs are native to semi-tropical climate, so needs a semi-tropical setup. Get glass aquariums that are tall and of not less than 10 gallon capacity. Glass aquariums can be cleaned easily and have a good visibility too. It should have a screen top and provide good ventilation. For the furniture of the enclosure, you can use cork, barks, sticks, branches etc. Before you place them in the cage, soak them in water containing a mild bleach solution overnight and let them dry completely to get devoid of any fungus. You can place live plant or fake plants inside the enclosure. If you are placing the sticks and wood pieces, then place them in a diagonal and slanting manner. Fill the enclosure with water that doesn't have chlorine and it needs to be replaced with fresh water every day. Place a bowl of 1-2 inches shallow with water. Store bought bowls look good and serve the purpose well.

Heat

Place heaters under the tank to provide heat to tree frogs.

These heaters need to be placed at either end of closure. For the heat to be absorbed place the rock on the area which is being heated. An alternate way to heat the enclosure is by placing the lamp on the high point of the enclosure. Make sure the lamp and the frog are separated by a screen cover.

Light

The frogs are nocturnal, so they will not be needing lighting of any kind.

Care

Tree frogs feed on insects. They will ingest small insects that fit their mouth size. Crickets are the best insects for feeding your tree frogs as they are available easily and easy to breed to feed your pet frogs. Let the insects remain enclosed for feeding. You can buy gut-loading food for the crickets. They are calcium rich, so tree frogs will get nutritious food when they feed on these crickets. Tree frog owners can also feed their frogs food that is coated with calcium and multivitamins 3 times per week to keep your tree frog healthy. Mist your tree frog everyday with water that has NO chlorine. Mornings is the best time for the job.

Cleaning Procedure

Milk frog / Trachycephalus resinifictrix

The enclosure needs to be cleaned well once a week. Take all the contents of the enclosure out, then rinse them and scrub them under hot water without using soap. When, you do the cleaning put the frogs in a small container. After cleaning the contents of the enclosure, you need to clean the tank well with hot water and the carpeting can be cleaned with laundry detergent and rinsed with clean water.

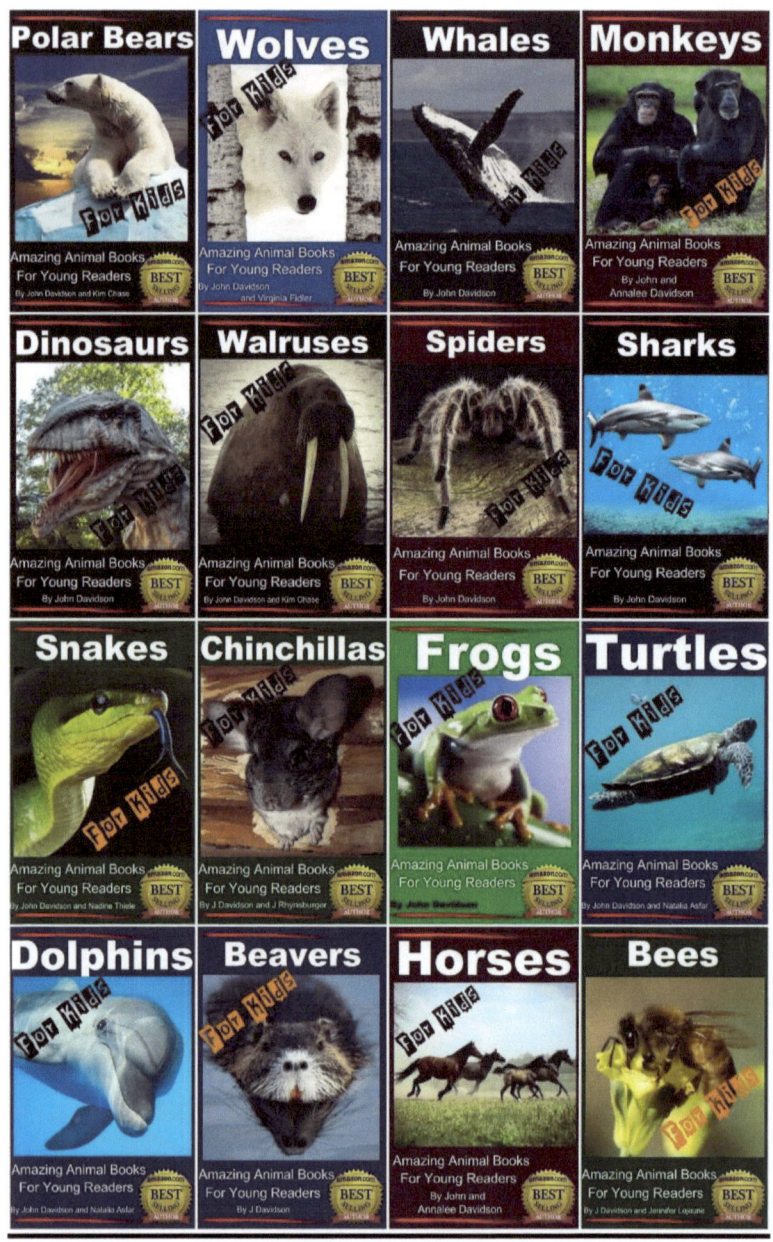

Purchase at Amazon.com
Website http://AmazingAnimalBooks.com

Top Ten Dog Breeds For Kids

Amazing Animal Books For Young Readers

Kisha Bennett & John Davidson

German Shepherds

Dog Books for Kids

K. Bennett

Bulldogs

Dog Books for Kids

K. Bennett

Dachshund

Dog Books for Kids

K. Bennett

Poodles

Labrador Retrievers

Dog Books for Kids

K. Bennett

Rottweilers

Dog Books for Kids

K. Bennett

Boxers

Dog Books for Kids

K. Bennett

Dog Books for Kids

K. Bennett

Golden Retrievers

Dog Books for Kids

K. Bennett

Puppies

Dog Books For Kids

Amazing Animal Books

By John Davidson

Beagles

Dog Books for Kids

K. Bennett

Yorkshire Terriers

Dog Books for Kids

K. Bennett

Dogs

Top Ten Dog Breeds For Kids

Amazing Animal Books For Young Readers

Zahra Jazieel & John Davidson

Cats For Kids

Amazing Animal Books For Young Readers

K. Bennett & John Davidson

Foxes For Kids

Amazing Animal Books For Young Readers

Zahra Jazieel & John Davidson

Wolves

For Kids

Amazing Animal Books For Young Readers

By John Davidson and Virginia Fidler

Our books are available at

1. Amazon.com
2. Barnes and Noble
3. Itunes
4. Kobo
5. Smashwords
6. Google Play Books

Download Free Books!
http://MendonCottageBooks.com

Publisher

JD-Biz Corp

P O Box 374

Mendon, Utah 84325

http://www.jd-biz.com/

Mendon Cottage Books

P O Box 374, Mendon Utah 84325

www.ingramcontent.com/pod-product-compliance
Lightning Source LLC
Chambersburg PA
CBHW040313010626
45792CB00022B/286